For Howard

Senior Moments
Poems

Table of Contents

Mixed Signals

I’m sitting at a stop sign
waiting for the light to change…
Just sitting at a stop sign
waiting for the light to change…
Why are those drivers
honking at me?
Why is it
they cannot see
that I’m sitting at this stop sign…

Oh, wait.
Time to move on.

Only on Thursdays

Senior day at the supermarket:
five percent off—worth the hassle.
But some are here for the company.
or for the prime rib dinner, available,
like the discount, only on Thursdays.

When the Phone Rings

Your grandchild (probably) is not in a
        Mexican prison,
nor even an American jail.
Your grandchild (probably) is not in a small
        town
in the Arizona desert, unable to leave
because of a broken axle—
especially if not old enough to drive,
nor with funds sufficient to buy a car.
Your grandchild (probably) is safe at home
        in bed,
almost certainly not in a Mexican prison.

Do not send money.

It's okay to call your grandchild's parent,
        though,
just to make sure.

A Matter of Time

How can it be that weeks fly by
and years so quickly go,
when every day is long
and every night more so?

Aging

I am old but my heart is young.
I wake each morning filled with hope,
out of habit, if nothing else.

All the English Majors

All the English majors
standing in a row
cannot stop the language
if it wants to grow.

And so new words are added,
and old words' meanings change
though some think it peculiar
and find the language strange.

Response to the Robocaller

Thanks, but no,
I do not need:
a back brace,
student loan relief,
another insurance policy,
consolidation of my credit card balance,
help with my computer.

Well, maybe help with my computer,
but, no, I won't give you access to it.
I think I will stick with the Geek Squad.

Senior Moments

If you have a senior moment
and it bothers you a lot,
just remember
what
you remember
and forget
what
you forgot.

Passengers on the No. 4 Bus

Boarding the bus at mid-morning
we're the only passengers under sixty,
the others mostly much older women.
They've outlived their men,
their children well past grown.
Wrinkled faces, sensible shoes,
large black bags.
They carry what they need.

If we could see inside
one of those bags we'd find:
something to read,
something to eat,
daily meds, plus
something for indigestion,
the list for today's shopping,
an odd glove perhaps and tokens.
Also pictures of loved ones—
grown up, dead, runaway among them—
faces unfamiliar now, even to her.

A Simple Pleasure

I bought a pink geranium
at the farm stand yesterday.
It makes me smile
to see it bloom
as I go about my day.

A Woman of Words

She sharpened pencils, knives, and tools,
and lots of other stuff.
She did not bother with her tongue,
for it was sharp enough.

Like a River

Like a river,
I have my highs and lows,
sometimes raging, rushing,
overflowing. Sometimes sluggish,
slow, unpleasant. But,
like a river, I am mostly
reliably steady and deep.

Like a river,
I am subject to storms
and lack of rain, or, in my case,
say, love, or appreciation,
as I am not actually a river,
only like one,
as I follow the course of my life.

Mirror Image

That wrinkled body,
those drooping breasts,
suggest her age
of many years.

She observes it
with the satisfaction
of a survivor
and reflects on how well
it has served her,
through the wear
and tear of years
and despite insults
to its integrity

She surveys all the scars:
some visible,
some not.

And she reflects on how,
touched by loving hands,
the body learns to love

and to accept love
in return.

He Thinks He Knows Her Now

After fifty years of marriage,
he thinks he knows her now:
the contours of her body,
her outline beneath the covers
as she sleeps;
her walk he recognizes
even from a distance.
He knows her likes and dislikes,
the meaning of her frowns,
what makes her laugh,
what makes her cry.
He knows her voice,
even the words she's likely to say.

Then he hears her express
an opinion he's not heard before,
on a subject she's never mentioned
in his hearing: a little known detail
about the French Revolution,
or an obscure quotation
from the Federalist papers.
He asks himself—and not for the first time—
who is this woman
to whom I have been married
for all these many years?

The Moon, the Mattress, and You

I recall moonlight pouring over us
on the mattress where we lay. It was
the only furnishing in the room,
before the prospect of visitors
shamed us into buying a bed.
The full moon kept us awake
for hours, something
calling to us in the moonlight.
Moon drenched sleep at last.

Not even the prospect of visitors
could shame us
into hanging curtains.

In My Dream Last Night

In my dream last night
we were young again,
yet blessed with wisdom
only age can bring.

We set out together,
my hand tucked
under your arm.

You wore a blue shirt,
and we were happy.

At the Senior Couples Exercise Class

The instructor mumbles.
Some are hard of hearing,
some merely inattentive.
The result is a less than routine
routine.

As some move left and others right,
some bend and twist and others stretch,
she finds her eyes turn toward him
and follows his example,
her body responding to his
as it has throughout the years.

The Lighthouse Keeper's Wife

The lighthouse keeper's wife
speaks after a long silence.
What stark loneliness!
What relentless sun!
What wild winds
and restless waves,
dark nights and silent days!

When first you brought me
to this desolate outcropping
of rock beyond the shore,
I was filled with the romance
of it all—being swept
off my feet and into
your steady arms and sturdy boat.

I could not have imagined
what it would be like
to live here alone with you
(before the children came,
of course,) Now they are grown
and gone, and not one drowned
as I had feared, but living
on solid ground somewhere far away.
Now we two are alone again.
I did not know what life
I chose—if I chose at all—
so long ago I don't remember.
What raw beauty!

the endless ocean,
the endless sky.
The endless tasks you face
keeping the light.
The endless love that makes it all
not only bearable, but somehow
a life to be desired.

On the Breaking of Spells

And why were we then out kissing toads
when princes were in short supply?
Would it have been better to sit in ashes,
waiting for fairy godmothers to liberate us?
Or to have slept one hundred years
        waiting
to be discovered and kissed?

Why could we not see what uncommon
        men
walked beside us on the common road,
and what uncommon women we might
        become,
merely by lifting up our eyes
to meet their guileless own?
Our glorious feet had no need
        of glass slippers;
we might have danced
as happily in peasant shoes.
We might have spent our nights
as fondly between rough-woven sheets.

All these years now have we lived
as honest cottagers and felt nobility and
        grace
transform our lives.
Our hearth fires keep us warm.
Sisters, has it not been ever so?

An Early Morning Long Ago

Six sleeping people
in a house on fire
awaken and escape
the flames somehow,
somehow resume their lives.

Only two remain now
to remember their mother,
standing barefoot
in a neighbor's yard,
wearing nothing
but her flimsy summer
nightgown.

On Memory

My sisters and I
make scrapbooks
for our mother,
so she will remember us
when we have grown up
and moved away.
We cut pictures from magazines
and the Sears Roebuck catalog
and use our white school paste
to put them in old ledgers
our granddaddy has given us.

She encourages the scrapbooks
but tries to reassure her daughters
that she would never forget us.

How could she?
How could anyone
forget her own children?

Her Sweet Daddy Cecil

"My sweet daddy Cecil died,"
she wrote in the notice
she sent to the papers.
Although I didn't know them,
I cried when I read the news.
Oh, I wept for Cecil
and his grieving daughter,
his ex-wife Alice and all the bereaved,
but more for myself
and my own sweet daddy,
and for all the daughters
of all the sweet daddies
who have died.

After a Phone Call in the Night

The dead are still dead
this morning,
despite our fitful sleep
and earnest, yearning
dreams…

The dead are still dead
this morning,
and we are broken,
still…

To a Long Time Friend Now Lost

Time and distance cause friendships
to fray, to break, unwind.
You chose not the long unwinding,
the loosening of strands braided
together through years of connecting
and reconnecting, of shared
experience that bound us together.
You chose instead to cut that cord,
leaving me holding the loose end
you chose to leave behind.

Grief, the Harvest

Grief is a knot in the chest,
an emptiness in the night,
a companion of the day.
grief washes over all,
then goes away, only
to return when least expected.

Another friend died yesterday.

Grief is the harvest of years
of loving and caring for others.
We now know that we will
mourn them all, except those few
who may linger long enough
to mourn for us.

Grief comes at night
and stays, a weight
In the chest, a longing
tinged with disbelief.
We wake to a new reality.

Another friend died yesterday.

The Old Man Sits by the Dying Fire

Six strong sons gone off to war
he sits alone in the quiet house
sees outside the field unplowed
feels inside the empty rooms
strains to hear the absent laughter
waits in vain for news from afar,
longs as ever
for their long-dead mother.

A Chill in the Night

I have felt the touch of death.
brushing past me in the night,
only passing by this time,
but taking note of my location,
sure to come this way again.

Let Winter Come

Let winter come:
a time to hibernate,
to keep warm, to tend
to our inner selves,
to reason things out,
to look at our lives’
balance sheet,
to build up a store
of love and hope
and resolve, to last
us through until spring.

At the Cemetery in Grady, Arkansas

My roots are here
in this green earth,
entwined with bones
of those long dead,
the pull that they
exert on me
not strong enough
to keep me here,
but too strong
to let me stay away.

Observation

Boat moves slowly down the river,
plane swoops low across the sky,
busses, trolleys, cars go by, as we
sit still amidst them, you and I.

Afterthought

The things I never said
(and might have)
come to me now with
haunting insistence.

The Crone Questions the Stereotype

Could wisdom really come with age,
regardless of one's circumstance,
or might one stay completely clueless,
none the wiser through the years,
experience teaching nothing much?

Last Drab Days of Winter

> "meanwhile the world goes on."
> --line from "Wild Geese" by Mary Oliver

Hearts are set on summer. Meanwhile
the last drab days of winter linger. The
gloom envelops all; the world
is shrouded in sodden gray. Time goes
slowly, and winter drags on.

Pandemic

Our retirement plans
did not include
this most disquieting
interlude.

We planned to travel,
to gad about,
spend time with friends,
eat dinner out.

Instead, we sit
and read our books,
give tv shows
second looks,

venture out to drug
and grocery store—
then stay at home
and not much more.

Wear a Mask When Out in Public

Eyes meet eyes
through sunglasses
on our afternoon walk.

We return his warm greeting,
and bid him a cheery
farewell. He says
"see you soon."

Once he's out of earshot
we turn to one another
and ask, as one:

"Who was that masked man?"

Sheltering in the Kitchen

We flatten the curve
but fatten ourselves,
taking pride in what we're
baking, eating it as we go.

Quarantine

Will we then
never dance again,
nor eat with friends
at a crowded table?

See grandchildren's
smiling faces,
feel our children's
warm embraces?

Lamentation

We rage for life that once we knew,
we long for those we cannot see,
we weep for lives that might be lost,
we mourn in fear of what might be.

Scrubs

This hospital's staff
wears scrubs
in a rainbow of colors.
There may be color coding,
but if so it isn't evident.
There's burgundy, rust
and navy, bright blue,
light blue, green,
and marigold.
Only her doctor, she observes,
wears marigold.

It is early in the morning,
but the doctor is sitting
in a chair by her bed,
wearing his marigold scrubs
when he tells her the Covid test
was negative.
She knows already, though:
no one is wearing protective gear
over their colorful scrubs.

Doctor's Orders

We stayed at home to flatten the curve
and handled our mail with deep suspicion.
We washed our hands and our veggies,
        too.
We didn't go out the whole week through.
That's what Dr. Fauci said to do.

We wore our masks when out of doors
and viewed our neighbors with suspicion.
How the virus spread nobody knew
we disinfected everything—old and new.
as Dr. Fauci said he'd do.

When we finally ventured out to shop
the empty shelves raised our suspicion.
Flour was scarce, paper towels were few.
They were out of toilet tissue, too.
What would Dr. Fauci do?

We worshipped, studied, and worked
        online,
and though some viewed it with suspicion,
we got absentee ballots and voted, too.
We limited celebrations to few,
as Dr. Fauci said he would do.

We didn't get our hair cut,
although we did see our physician.

We went to the drug store a time or twoand got
our shots for shingles and flu,
just as Dr. Fauci said to do.

When Covid vaccines were approved,
though many viewed them with suspicion,
We got shot one and then shot two.
It seemed the prudent thing to do,
and Dr. Fauci got his, too.

We took our masks off out of doors
and eyed our neighbors with recognition.
We hugged our kids and grandkids, too,
as we had longed so long to do,
and Dr. Fauci told us too.

In Times of Plague and Insurrection

In times of plague and insurrection
what's important is clear,
making one wonder how
we have escaped understanding
for so long the simple,
complicated truth
that only love can save us now.

Acknowledgments

The poem *Observation* appeared on DASH busses and the King Street Trolley in Alexandria, Virginia, as part of the Alexandria Transit Company's 2017 DASHing Words in Motion competition, in *Elderberries*, and in an exhibit sponsored by At Home in Alexandria.

Many of these poems were started (or finished!) in workshops led by Wendy Kaplan, then Poet Laureate of Alexandria; KaNikki Jakarta, First Black Poet Laureate of Alexandria, *Write Like a Woman*; Lisa Colburn, *Market Street Writers*; and Summer Hardinge, *Writing Beyond Margins*. I am grateful beyond measure to them and to participants in the workshops for their inspiration and affirmation.

My deep appreciation goes to my dear friend Marge Corletti, who has offered encouragement, suggestions, and always gentle critique as I wrote these poems and selected them for publication. She has never declined being first (or second) reader, even when she suspects she may be asked to read different versions of the same poem over and over. I am more grateful to her than I can ever say.

My husband, Howard Middleton, in addition to inspiring some of the poems and taking the picture on the back cover, has been a faithful and careful reader throughout the process. I am deeply grateful for this and for his companionship and love. I want to remind him—and inform any curious reader—that it's poetry, not biography.

About the Author

Betty Jo Middleton has been writing poems almost all her life, but this is her first chapbook of poetry. In recent years her poems have appeared on DASH busses and the King Street Trolley in Alexandria, Virginia, as part of the Alexandria Transit Company's DASHing Words in Motion competition; in a virtual visual *Speak Your Truth /Black Lives Matter* exhibit hosted by the Northern Virginia Fine Arts Association's Athenaeum gallery; in newspapers and newsletters, and in the anthology *Meditations on Class.* A song based on her poem is in this anthology also. She is the author of *To Touch Inward Springs: Teaching and Learning for Faith Development.*

She has been married since 1965 to J. Howard Middleton. They have two children and four grandchildren. They live in Alexandria, Virginia.

Made in the USA
Middletown, DE
17 October 2022